PON

P9-EEI-730

MATH IN OUR WORLD

MULTIPLY
TO MAKE PARTY PLANS

By Linda Bussell

Reading consultant: Susan Nations, M.Ed.,
author/literacy coach/consultant in literacy development
Math consultant: Rhea Stewart, M.A., mathematics content specialist

WEEKLY READER®
PUBLISHING

Please visit our web site at www.garethstevens.com
For a free color catalog describing our list of high-quality books,
call 1-800-542-2595 (USA) or 1-800-387-3178 (Canada). Our fax: 1-877-542-2596

Library of Congress Cataloging-in-Publication Data

Bussell, Linda.
        Multiply to make party plans / by Linda Bussell.
            p. cm. — (Math in our world level 3)
        Includes bibliographical references and index.
        ISBN-10: 0-8368-9285-2 — ISBN-13: 978-0-8368-9285-7 (lib. bdg.)
        ISBN-10: 0-8368-9384-0 — ISBN-13: 978-0-8368-9384-7 (softcover)
        1. Multiplication—Juvenile literature. I. Title.
    QA115.B88 2008
    513.2'13—dc22   2008013129

This edition first published in 2009 by
Weekly Reader® Books
An Imprint of Gareth Stevens Publishing
1 Reader's Digest Road
Pleasantville, NY 10570-7000 USA

Creative Director: Lisa Donovan
Production Designer: Amy Ray, Studio Montage
Copy Editor: Susan Labella
Photo Researcher: Kim Babbitt

Photo Credits: cover, title page: Digital Vision/Getty Images; pp. 4–5, 10, 14, 15, 20–21: Russell Pickering;
p. 6, 7, 8, 13, 16: Hemera Technologies; p. 11: Photodisc; p. 17: Bill Aron/Photo Edit, p. 19: BananaStock

Printed in the United States

1 2 3 4 5 6 7 8 9 10 09 08

Table of Contents

Words that appear in the glossary are printed in **boldface** type the first time they occur in the text.

Chapter 1

Sandwich Multiplication

The students in the chorus club are excited! Their teachers just told them good news. Mr. Sanchez and Miss Anderson say they are having a party. Mr. Sanchez says that students will plan the party. Parents will help.

Miss Anderson asks the students what kind of party they want. The students choose a picnic. They will have it at a park. They will decorate. They will have food and games. It will be fun.

Students will decorate for the party.

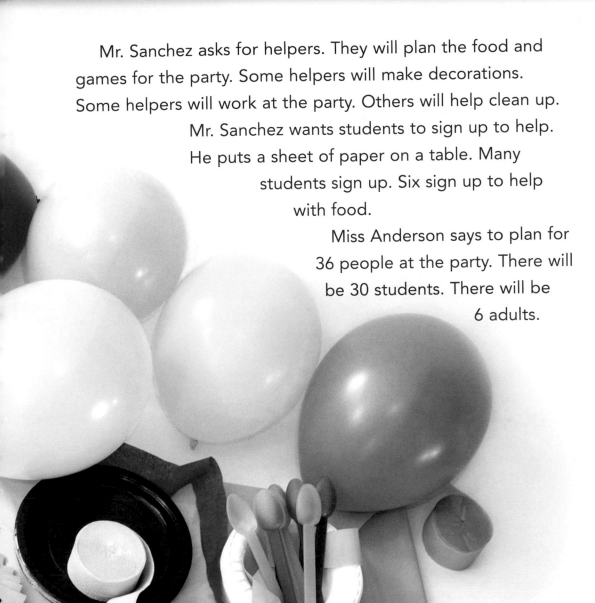

Mr. Sanchez asks for helpers. They will plan the food and games for the party. Some helpers will make decorations. Some helpers will work at the party. Others will help clean up.

Mr. Sanchez wants students to sign up to help. He puts a sheet of paper on a table. Many students sign up. Six sign up to help with food.

Miss Anderson says to plan for 36 people at the party. There will be 30 students. There will be 6 adults.

Mike and Kayla will help with the food. They want to make sandwiches. Mike's favorite is turkey on a bun. Kayla's favorite is cheese on bread. They decide to make those two kinds of sandwiches. How many of each do they need?

To find out, they ask for a vote. Each student in the 30-member club votes for one sandwich. Including Mike, 20 students want turkey on a bun. The rest, including Kayla, want cheese on bread.

Kayla subtracts.

30 − 20 = 10

There are 30 students in the club. Kayla knows that 20 students want turkey on a bun. She figures out that 10 students want cheese on bread. She says that 2 times as many students want turkey as cheese.

Mr. Sanchez says to plan the same for adults.

There are 6 adults. There should be 4 turkey sandwiches and 2 cheese sandwiches for them.

Now Kayla and Mike can make a shopping list.

Sandwiches

	Turkey	Cheese
Students	20	10
Adults	+ 4	+ 2
Total	24	12

Kayla and Mike ask Mike's mom to help. They must figure out how much food to buy. They need enough food to make 24 turkey sandwiches. They need enough to make 12 cheese sandwiches.

Mike's mom can buy turkey in packs of 10 **servings**. Mike and Kayla **multiply**. They can make 24 sandwiches with 3 packs. They will have 6 servings left.

If they use packs with 8 servings, they still need 3 packs. They will have no turkey left. If they use packs with 12 servings, they will need only 2 packs.

3 packages of 10 servings	$3 \times 10 = 30$	6 left over
3 packages of 8 servings	$3 \times 8 = 24$	0 left over
2 packages of 12 servings	$2 \times 12 = 24$	0 left over

Buns are often sold in packs of 8. Mike's mom says they will need 3 packs. That makes 24 sandwiches. If they find buns in packs of 12, they will need only 2 packs.

Now they know how much food to buy to make 24 turkey sandwiches. Mike adds this information to a shopping list.

Next, Mike and Kayla decide how much bread and cheese to buy.

Needed to Make 24 Turkey Sandwiches

Turkey		
3 packages of 10 servings	$3 \times 10 = 30$	6 left over
3 packages of 8 servings	$3 \times 8 = 24$	0 left over
2 packages of 12 servings	$2 \times 12 = 24$	0 left over
Buns		
3 packages of 8 servings	$3 \times 8 = 24$	0 left over
2 packages of 12 servings	$2 \times 12 = 24$	0 left over

Mike and Kayla need 12 cheese sandwiches. Mike says he puts 2 slices of cheese on a sandwich. They will need 24 slices of cheese.

12 × 2 = 24

Cheese comes in packs of 10 slices. They will need 3 packs. Three packs have 30 slices in all.

3 × 10 = 30

There will be 6 cheese slices left over.

30 − 24 = 6

Mike's mom makes sandwiches for a snack.

Kayla and Mike are hungry. Mike's mom makes them sandwiches.

Kayla reads the bread label. There are 15 slices in a **loaf**. They will need 2 loaves. There will be 6 slices of bread left over.

They will have enough food to make 3 more cheese sandwiches. Mike says this is okay. Some people might eat more than one sandwich.

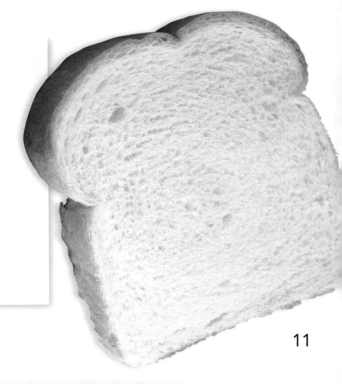

Bread:
2 loaves of 15 slices
$15 + 15 = 30$ 6 left over

Cheese:
3 packages of 10 servings
$3 \times 10 = 30$ 6 left over

Mike finishes the shopping list. He is ready to go to the store with his mom and Kayla.

Shopping List

Turkey:
  2 packages of 12 servings (24 servings)
  OR
  3 packages of 8 servings (24 servings)
  OR
  3 packages of 10 servings (30 servings)

Buns:
  2 packages of 12 servings (24 servings)
  OR
  3 packages of 8 servings (24 servings)

Cheese:
  3 packages of cheese (30 slices)

Bread:
  2 loaves of bread (30 slices)

Chapter 2

Salad Toss-Up!

Maria and Claire help with food for the picnic, too. They want to make a salad. Maria says her family has a recipe for good fruit salad. Everyone loves it. Her dad will help make the salad.

Maria and Claire go to the kitchen. Maria finds the recipe for the fruit salad. It has strawberries, bananas, oranges, apples, and grapes in it. Claire says the salad sounds good!

Fruit Salad (4 servings)

1 apple   6 strawberries
1 banana   8 grapes
1 orange

Wash fruit.
Have an adult slice the banana, apple, orange,
and strawberries. Place in bowl. Add grapes.
Mix with spoon. Chill.

Claire and Maria need 36 servings of salad for the party. Maria's recipe makes only 4 servings.

Claire says they must multiply everything in the recipe by 9. Then they will have enough fruit salad.

9 × 4 = 36

Claire and Maria read the recipe together. They multiply each ingredient by 9. Claire makes a shopping list. She lists each item they need. Maria's dad will take them to the store.

Claire and Maria use the recipe to make a shopping list.

Shopping List

9 apples

9 bananas

9 oranges

54 strawberries

72 grapes

Chapter 3

Thirst Quenchers

Jacob and Carlos help plan the party. They are in charge of drinks.

Jacob says they should buy 2 drinks for each person. The weather will be hot. People will play games. Everyone will be thirsty.

Carlos thinks they should buy water. Maybe they should buy juice, too. Carlos and Jacob decide to buy juice and water. They will buy extra water. That way, they will not run out of drinks.

Carlos thinks they should have plenty of water for everyone.

The store sells six-packs of juice. Carlos and Jacob will buy 6 six-packs.

6 × 6 = 36

The store sells **cases** of water. There are 24 bottles in a case. They will buy 2 cases.

24 + 24 = 48

Carlos says 2 cases will give them 12 extra bottles of water.

48 − 36 = 12

That will be enough to drink.

Now the food for the picnic is planned. They will serve sandwiches, salad, and drinks.

Shopping
List

6 six-packs of juice (36 servings)
2 cases of water (48 servings)

Chapter 4

Party Day!

The day of the picnic is here! Everyone worked hard to plan and prepare. The decoration team made bright banners. They decorated the tables. The game team planned many games.

The weather is perfect. It is sunny and warm. Everyone enjoys the games. They play very hard. Soon they are thirsty. Jacob and Carlos offer water from a cooler.

At last, it is time to eat.

Kayla and Mike help the parents serve sandwiches. Claire and Maria scoop fruit salad onto plates. Jacob and Carlos hand out drinks.

People talk and laugh. There is plenty to eat. Everyone has a great time.

Now it is time to clean up. Mr. Sanchez thanks the teams for their help. Miss Anderson says that their planning made the picnic fun. The students smile. They are the perfect party planners!

Everything is ready for the picnic.

What Did You Learn?

① There are 8 slices of cheese in a package. Jim has 3 friends for lunch. Jim and his friends each want 2 slices of cheese for their sandwiches. How many slices will they use?

② Hot dogs come in a package of 8. Tom's mother bought 2 packages of hot dogs. How many hot dogs can she serve?

Use a separate piece of paper.

Glossary

✗ (multiplication sign): a symbol placed between two numbers to show that the first number is to be multiplied by the second number

Example: $2 \times 3 = 6$

case: a container of like things packaged together, such as a case of water bottles

loaf: bread or other food that is baked in one piece and then sliced into smaller pieces

multiply: to add the same number to itself one or more times

serving: an amount of food for one person

Index

About the Author

Linda Bussell has written and designed books, supplemental learning materials, educational games, and software programs for children and young adults. She lives with her family in San Diego, California.